Forest Fires

Michele Ingber Drohan

The Rosen Publishing Group's
PowerKids Press™
New York

Published in 1999 by The Rosen Publishing Group, Inc.
29 East 21st Street, New York, NY 10010

First Edition

Book Design: Danielle Primiceri

Photo Credits: Cover © ; p. 5 © Gianni Dagli Orti/Corbis; p. 6 © Wayne Aldridge/International Stock; p. 9 © Smith, Clyde H./FPG International; p. 10 © Dennie Cody/FPG International; p. 13 © Scott Barrow/International Stock; p. 14 © Robert Graham/FPG International; p. 17 © Jeff and Alexa Henry; p. 18 © Bob Firth/International Stock; p. 21 © 1997 Digital Vision Ltd.

Drohan, Michele Ingber.
    Forest fires / by Michele Ingber Drohan.
        p.   cm.— (Natural disasters)
    Includes index.
    Summary: Discusses different kinds of forest fires, what causes them, where they occur, and how they can be prevented.
    ISBN 0-8239-5287-8
    1. Forest fires—Juvenile literature. 2. Forest fires—Prevention and control—Juvenile literature. 3. Forest fires—United States—Juvenile literature.
4. Forest fires—United States—Prevention and control—Juvenile literature. [1. Forest fires.] I. Title. II. Series: Drohan, Michele Ingber. Natural disasters.
SD421.23.D76 1998
363.37'9—dc21
                        98-9260
                        CIP
                        AC

Manufactured in the United States of America

Contents

The Myth of Fire

Fire has always been important to people. Many people think fire is **sacred** (SAY-kred). This is because it gives warmth, but it can also cause harm. Many different **cultures** (KUL-cherz) all over the world have **myths** (MITHS) about fire. Myths are stories. Some myths tell how things in nature came to be.

The most famous myth about fire comes from ancient Greece. This myth tells of how fire was stolen from the **gods** (GODZ) who ruled over Earth and then given to humans. Today we know that fire is something that happens in nature. And it was on Earth long before people were.

This work of art shows the ancient Greek myth of Prometheus giving ▶ fire to humans after he stole it from the gods.

What Is Fire?

Fire is the **flame** (FLAYM), heat, and light that we see when something is burning. Fire needs three things to burn. These things are a gas called **oxygen** (AHK-sih-jin), **fuel** (FYOOL), and heat. Oxygen comes from the air we breathe. Fuel comes from things that burn, such as wood, leaves, and paper. When oxygen and fuel mix with heat, a fire starts.

Fire is very useful. We cook food with it, and it heats our homes. But fire is also very **powerful** (POW-er-ful). It can be **dangerous** (DAYN-jer-us) when it gets out of control.

◄ *Even though fire is beautiful and helps us in many ways, we always have to be careful when we are around it.*

How Does a Forest Fire Start?

Forest fires can start in different ways. Sometimes they are started by natural causes. This can happen when lightning hits a tree in a forest and starts a fire. This occurs a lot because there are more than 40,000 lightning storms each year all over the world.

But most forest fires are started by people. In fact, four out of every five forest fires are caused by people. If someone doesn't put out a cigarette or if a campfire is left burning by a camper, a forest fire can start easily. If people were more careful, we could **prevent** (pre-VENT) most forest fires.

Fire can destroy huge areas of land and trees in a very short period of time. ▶

Types of Forest Fires

There are three types of forest fires. A ground fire burns slowly. It moves along the ground using leaves and moss as fuel. You don't see many flames in a ground fire. You might only see glowing **embers** (EM-berz) on the forest floor. A surface fire burns more quickly. It also stays close to the ground. But it uses branches as fuel, and it can burn and kill trees. A crown fire is the worst kind of fire. It climbs up trees and moves very fast. Crown fires move from treetop to treetop—as fast as ten miles an hour!

◀ *Surface fires can move quickly and are often spread by wind.*

Brush Fires

Brush fires are a special type of fire. They race across open land in hot, dry areas and burn almost everything in their paths. When the weather is hot and dry in a place with lots of fuel, such as dry grasses and bushes, a brush fire will start.

Many people have built homes on dry land that used to be wild. This is because wildland is very beautiful. But there is a high risk of fire in these areas. As more people move into these areas, they risk losing their homes and other buildings to fire. In 1991 a brush fire burned thousands of homes and buildings in Oakland, California. Twenty-six people died.

These firefighters are watching a brush fire to see which way it might move. ▶

Fighting Fire

When firefighters get to a forest fire, they must think about where the fire might go and how quickly it will move. We know that fire needs three things to burn: oxygen, fuel, and heat. Firefighters need to remove at least one of these things to put out the fire.

First, the firefighters make a fire line. A fire line is a line made in the ground by clearing away all the fuel, such as leaves and branches. If all the fuel is taken away, the fire cannot spread. A fire line must be wide enough to contain the fire. If it's windy, a fire can jump over the line and spread. Firefighters use tools, such as special axes called **Pulaskis** (puh-LAS-keez), to dig fire lines. Next, firefighters spray lots of cold water on the fire to remove the heat.

Fighting forest fires is hard work. Sometimes firefighters have to work for several days or weeks to stop a fire.

Smoke Jumpers

Sometimes a fire is in a **remote** (rih-MOHT) area. This can make it hard for firefighters to reach the fire by truck. And it may take days to reach it on foot. In 1940 the United States Forest Service started using smoke jumpers. Smoke jumpers are firefighters who **parachute** (PAYR-uh-shoot) out of airplanes and land on the ground near the fire. Other parachutes carrying **supplies** (suh-PLYZ), such as Pulaskis, are sent down with them. If firefighters get to the fire early, they can stop it sooner.

Smoke jumping is very dangerous. Smoke jumpers are specially trained so that they don't get hurt when they are doing their job.

Not only do smoke jumpers have to be skilled firefighters, but they also have to be willing to jump out of a plane to get to a fire! ▶

Yellowstone Fire Season

Every summer Yellowstone National Park has a fire season. Many fires start from lightning in the hot, dry weather. The 1988 season was the worst fire season in history. There were 249 fires in the park. About 25,000 firefighters worked all summer, day and night, to stop the fires. Airplanes and helicopters were used to drop water on the fires from above.

The fires were finally put out by an early snowfall. About 1 million acres of Yellowstone had burned. Many people were upset at the loss of parts of this beautiful park. The worst fire that season wasn't caused by lightning. It was caused by people.

◄ *This helicopter is dropping water on part of Yellowstone National Park to stop a forest fire from spreading.*

Let It Burn?

In 1972 the National Park Service created a "Let Burn" plan for national parks such as Yellowstone. This means that any fire started by natural causes will be allowed to burn until it goes out on its own. This is because fires are a part of a forest's natural **ecosystem** (EE-koh-SIS-tum). When natural fires are stopped by firefighters, changes can occur in the forest that **threaten** (THREH-tun) the future of the forest. The forest may have trouble **protecting** (pruh-TEK-ting) itself from future fires. But many people don't like the Let Burn plan because it takes years for new trees to grow again after a fire.

Some fires are actually good for trees and nature. A burned forest may look ugly at first, but after a while beautiful new trees will grow. ▶

Protecting Your Home

You may live in an area where forest or brush fires happen often. There are things you and your family can do to protect your home. Be sure to keep dead branches and leaves away from your house. The **shingles** (SHING-gulz) on the roof should be made of fireproof material. And with your family, decide on a special meeting place. If there is a fire, and you get separated from your family, you'll know to meet at that place. It's also important never to play with matches or fire—no matter where you are. Fire is very powerful. Remember what Smokey Bear says: "Only you can prevent forest fires."

Web Sites:

You can learn more about forest fires at this Web site: http://www.fema.gov/kids/

Glossary

culture (KUL-cher) The beliefs, customs, art, and religions of a group of people.

dangerous (DAYN-jer-us) Something that can cause harm.

ecosystem (EE-koh-SIS-tum) The special way that plants and animals function together in nature.

ember (EM-ber) A piece of wood that glows in the ashes of a fire.

flame (FLAYM) The glowing light that rises up from a fire.

fuel (FYOOL) Anything that can be burned.

god (GOD) A being or object that is thought to have more power than humans.

myth (MITH) A story that tells how things in nature were made.

oxygen (AHK-sih-jin) A colorless gas that makes up part of the air we breathe.

parachute (PAYR-uh-shoot) To jump out of an airplane with an umbrella-like object on your back.

powerful (POW-er-ful) Strong.

prevent (pre-VENT) To keep something from happening.

protect (pruh-TEKT) To keep from harm.

Pulaski (puh-LAS-kee) A tool that looks like an ax and a hoe that is used by firefighters to make a fire line.

remote (rih-MOHT) Far away.

sacred (SAY-kred) Something that is highly respected and very important.

shingle (SHING-gul) A thin piece of material that covers the roof of a house.

supplies (suh-PLYZ) The things a person needs to do a job.

threaten (THREH-tun) To be a possible cause of harm.

Index

B
brush fire, 12, 22

C
campfire, 8
cigarette, 8
crown fire, 11
culture, 4

D
dangerous, 7, 16

E
ecosystem, 20
embers, 11

F
firefighters, 15, 16, 19, 20
fire line, 15
flame, 7, 11
fuel, 7, 11, 12, 15

G
gods, 4
ground fire, 11

H
heat, 7, 15

L
lightning, 8, 19

M
materials, 22
myth, 4

O
oxygen, 7, 15

P
parachute, 16
parks, 19, 20
powerful, being, 7, 22

prevention, 8, 22
protecting, 20, 22
Pulaski, 15, 16

R
remote, 16

S
sacred, 4
shingles, 22
smoke jumpers, 16
Smokey Bear, 22
supplies, 16
surface fire, 11

T
threaten, 20

Y
Yellowstone National Park, 19, 20

24